Thou Art an Inspiration, Be an Inspiration

Albert Walters

authorHOUSE®

AuthorHouse™
1663 Liberty Drive
Bloomington, IN 47403
www.authorhouse.com
Phone: 1 (800) 839-8640

Published by AuthorHouse 06/08/2016

ISBN: 978-1-5246-0662-6 (sc)
ISBN: 978-1-5246-0661-9 (e)

Library of Congress Control Number: 2016907129

Print information available on the last page.

Any people depicted in stock imagery provided by Thinkstock are models, and such images are being used for illustrative purposes only. Certain stock imagery © Thinkstock.

This book is printed on acid-free paper.

Because of the dynamic nature of the Internet, any web addresses or links contained in this book may have changed since publication and may no longer be valid. The views expressed in this work are solely those of the author and do not necessarily reflect the views of the publisher, and the publisher hereby disclaims any responsibility for them.

A Review Of Our Legacy

by Albert Walters

It is a blessed person who chooses the way of the Lord. So I thank God for Rosa Parks and Martin Luther King, Jr. Choosing the way of life they did at that early stage, cherishing that frame of mind and upholding that focus to serve God and their fellow men. Brothers and Sisters to me this great accomplishment of them both was a manifestation of God. He used them greatly for us to see and understand that He is a loving, merciful father and friend who is still alive and is still in full control. That should neither be slighted nor mocked. He has a perfect plan and timing in all of our lives. He simply requires us to serve him in spirit and in truth.

To me, Martin Luther King, Jr. and Rosa Parks should be remembered for their gallant efforts and sacrifices they made in their quest for peace in the world. They stood up bravely at the boycotting of the buses, they stood up bravely against segregation opposing its oppression. And through it all, together gallantly they both gained their most prestigious prize, the victory for unity to bond us all more together as one.

MOTHER AFRICA

By: ALBERT W. WALTERS

Isaiah 35v1-4 The wilderness and the solitary place shall be glad for them; and the desert shall rejoice, and bloom as the rose. It shall blossom abundantly. And rejoice even with joy and singing: Mother Africa God has truly blessed thee, and I hail thy most precious name, I am hoping and praying that some day, some sweet day you shall brake forth blooming beautiful as the rose and this is my song and my prayer to thee.

Mother Africa surely the cattle on a thousand hills are thine, the tall evergreen trees looking over the mountain streams and the song birds singing ever so sweetly their lullabies are thine. O mother Africa my heart mind body and soul yearn for thee. O, I am mesmerized over the thought of loosing you,

Mother Africa I have got you on my mind and there you shall ever be, no one can take your place no one ever will. O you are so beautiful and precious o yes you are beautiful and priceless a treasure to me. 1 John 4v7-8 Beloved let us love one another: for love is of God; and every one that loveth is born of God, and knoweth God. He that loveth not knoweth not God; for God is love.

Mother Africa my heart is filled with love and praises for thee, and it shall ever be, and as a song and a prayer I am hoping someday some sweet day you shall break forth blooming beautifully as the rose. A writer once said, "Love swells like the waves of the sea but ebbs like its tide," but loving father Jesus, like a rose trampled on the ground, you took the fall because of your love for me, how could I but be forever grateful unto you. O please keep me in that frame of mind ever to be grateful unto you. The sweetest sound I can ever hear is the lifting of thy name in glory, honour and praise. O what a glorious day that will be when we meet on that beautiful shore.

Exodus 15v11 who is like unto thee, O Lord, among the gods? Who is like thee glorious in holiness, fearful in praises, doing wonders?

IF THY LOVE BE MINE

If thy love be mine, I'd give praises; yea, I'd give endless
praises to my Lord and King for creating you;
And O, so good and true Thank Him for answering my
prayer, my fondest dream, my heart's desire.

Well Beloved, if thy love be mine, with a joyful heart I'd
cleave to
thee, and pledge to thee my life;
My heart an open book. Forever more this will be,
I'd ne'er decline one measure.

Mountains may crumble, empires may fall but beloved,
I wonder what fate could withstand our love,
If in Unity we stand what sound could I hear
That could thrill me more? What beauty could I behold
that could charm me more? For thou art
the fairest of ten thousand to my soul.

Precious thy stature and perfect thy frame shall ever remain

O, with an ember of thy love thou hast engraved on my heart a
song, a new song, a song that shall never grow old.
O, a song that blesses my soul.

If thy love be mine? That will be the day,
That'll be the day when I say "Goodbye world' I'm gone.
I'm gone to a new world a fairer world on high
Happy to be ever with my love." O, no other love have I.

God believes in you.

****

By A. W. Walters

LIFE CAN BE BEAUTIFUL

Albert Walters

As you live, you will learn that some
people are free and some are
bound within this vast great world around
us. But I have a dream deeply
rooted within the celestial realm that
there is a brighter side somewhere.
Never stop until you find it! Oh yes, there
is a brighter side somewhere.

"Foxes have holes, birds their nest, but
the sons of man have nowhere
to rest." Well brothers and sisters, beloved
friends, why regret? Why be a
beggar whose only dream will not come
true. Sail on sailor. Whatever the
tide may be, may your shores never grow
old and love always guide you.

A writer once said, "I have learned that
success is to be measured not
so much by the position that one has
reached in life, as by the obstacles
which he has overcome while trying to
succeed." by, Booker T Washington
1856.
There is a way that seems right unto man,
but the ends thereof are the ways
of death. Let no one's motives be yours.
Friends, there is a race to be run and

a victory to be won. Oh how highly favored
art thou among ten thousands;
this whole world is a stage and thou art
an actor. Whatsoever thy hand
findeth to do, do it with thy might; for
there is no work, nor device, nor
knowledge, nor wisdom in the grave when thou goest.

Life can be beautiful dear friends, but
it's just endeavor awaits our
positive response at work, at rest and at
play throughout our life's span.
Friends, smile a while and give your face
a rest. "Although in this world of
turmoil we live, there is nothing we cannot
master because the battle is the
Lord's." 2 Chronicles 20:15
Behold those happy harvesters that
Mother Nature has availed for
thee. Oh how intriguing and priceless a
treasure to me they seem to be. The
lovely sunshine giving thee warmth, the
pretty flowers with their delicate
fragrances, the towering evergreen trees
that slumber in the breeze,

Oh I wonder if King Solomon arrayed
more than any of these.
Oh how sweetly as a song this always will
resound, sowing good seeds on
good grounds, meeting friends and greeting
them. Oh my, Brothers, sisters
and beloved friends. Big day dawns
considering how wonderfully and

perfectly God has created us and into His
own image. O what great and
unmerited blessing God has bestowed upon
us. He is the sustainer of all our
blessings and His love and tender mercies endures forever.
My spiritual awakening: Knowing
where I am coming from and
where I am going. Accepting Jesus as my
personal Savior and humbling
myself to the leading of His Holy Spirit
has made me so consoled today.
And knowing that He has a perfect plan
and a perfect timing in my life is
actually living a purpose driven life. It has
left me singing a new song. I am
a new creation!

Acknowledging how fortunate I am
being a child of God and a good
ambassador in service for Him. 2 Timothy
2:15 says, "Be diligent to present
yourself approved to God as a workman
who does not need to be ashamed,
handling accurately the word of truth."

Matthew 5:14; "Ye are the light of the
world. A city that is set on a hill
cannot be hid." God bless America land
that I love. America is looked upon
as a role model around the world by many
less fortunate countries and God
has richly blessed them for their good deeds.
America keeps hope alive. Our

younger ones need much more enlightening
of God's words and song's that
lifts His Holy name mandatory in schools.
We need to keep our young ones
out of prisons confinements and teach
them and guide them toward a
brighter and a much more prosperous world of tomorrow.

A writer once said, through the guiding
light of wisdom and understanding
shall a family endure and children grow
strong in the security of the home
for they are the hope of the future. We
need social workers for the early
beginners and their parents for helping them in their needs.
Philippians 2:5 says, "Let this mind be
in you, which was also in Christ
Jesus."

To whom much is given much is required.
We are joint heirs with Christ
who is our bigger brother. Why not stand
up and be counted as a worthy
elect of our Lord, who is the sustainer of
all our blessings. And give Him all
the glory, honor and praise He is most
worthy of. His love and tender
mercies endures forever.

God said, "Love thy neighbor as thy self.
Do unto others as you would have
them do unto you. Fear not the one that
can destroy the body, but fear Him

who can destroy both body and soul. God
is a Holy Spirit that dwells within
our hearts. Depending on how we cherish
the thought of Him dwelling
within us, making ourselves willing and
available in service for Him. He
blesses us accordingly.

God should not be slighted neither should He be mocked!
Brothers and sisters, beloved friends, I am
totally baffled! Why is it that unto
this day, God's commands has not been
honored? Luke 2:14 says, "Let there
be peace on earth and goodwill towards men."

Psalm 127:1 says, "Unless the Lord
builds the house, they labor in
vain who build it; unless the Lord guards
the city, the watchman stays awake
in vain." Proverbs 29:18 says, "Where there
is no vision, the people perish:
but he that keepeth the law, happy is he."
The more we are together the
happier we shall be. God is coming back
for His perfect world and would
rather have it that way. Psalm 105:15:
"Touch not my anointed nor do my
prophets no harm!"

Brothers and Sisters, wise men still seek
Jesus. Teach a wise man, and he
will yet be wiser. Oh where is HE? Where
is my beloved, my sweet Rose of

Sharon who pleaded for me in Gethsemane
and paid my debt on Calvary?
Oh who am I that a king should bleed
and die for? And pleaded, "Not my
will but thine for"? The answer I may never
know why He ever loved me so,
but to that old rugged cross He went for me.

1 Corinthians 15:58: "Therefore, my
beloved brethren, be steadfast,
immovable, always abounding in the work
of the Lord, knowing that your
labor is not in vain in the Lord."

Galatians 6:9: "Let us not become weary
in doing good, for at the proper
time we will reap a harvest if we do not give up."

How great is our God! How great is His
name. He is the greatest one and
forever shall be the same. Oh great is
thy faithfulness Lord unto me.
Matthew 25:21 says, "Well done, thou
good and faithful servant: thou hast
been faithful over a few things, I will
make thee ruler over many things:
enter thou into the joy of thy Lord."

WHO BUILT THE MOUNTAINS

O precious memories floods my soul when ever I recall
where love and mercy found me,
where the bright and morning star
sheds its beams around me. O who built the mountains, those
beautiful mountains, and build them so high,
built them such firm structure that generations rely.
O who bids thee come, come be with me
where life is so full and all is free.
Come be with me
where there's never a venture awaits thee.

— — — — — — — — — — **0** — — — — — — — — — —

Friends, smile a while and give your face a rest
although in this world of turmoil we live
there's nothing we cannot master with the help
of that one that giveth thee strength.
Behold those happy harvesters that mother nature
has avail for thee, O how intriguing
and priceless a treasure to me they seem to be.
The lovely sunshine giving thee warmth,
the pretty flowers with their delicate fragrances,
the towering evergreen trees that slumber in the breeze,
O I wonder was King Soloman arrayed
more than any of these.

— — — — — — — — — — **0** — — — — — — — — — —

O how tall the mountains, how high the sky.
O how vast the ocean of love has avail to you and I.
O come be with me, come be with me,
where such rivers of delight I see,
the evergreen trees grow tall and the wind blows free,
come be with me where the cold water streams,
to the rivers flow, hence - those mighty timber trees,
the willow, the oak, the pine and so many of such do grow.
The explorers, the scientists, the archaeologists they all do go.
Friend, come be with me where no venture awaits thee.

– – – – – – – – – – 0 – – – – – – – – – –

Well friends, as there's a race to be run, and a prize to be won,
I wonder towards that great and final day when
we all shall be judged by our master for the
deeds we have done.
I wonder friend, because there won't be any excuse and
there won't be any escapes
for we have all been too long warned.
You can treasure your wealth, your diamonds, your gold,
but (friends again be warned),
they won't save your poor wicked soul.
It is easier for a camel to go through a needle's eye, than
for a rich man to enter into the kingdom of God.

– – – – – – – – – – 0 – – – – – – – – – –

Friend, as man to man is unjust and
there isn't a faithful one in whom you can trust,
why not heed your master's calling
who bids thee come and be at rest?
Beloved, He is a friend and a precious friend.
O as the clock ticks away each minute of the day

and seeing the trains running down the railroad track,
I wonder where are we going to run,
where are we going to hide, to whom are we going to cry,
when our loving master returns to claim His very own
if by His will and commands we do not abide.

— — — — — — — — — — **0** — — — — — — — — — —

O! I want to see Him to behold His beautiful face;
to give Him my tribute in praises,
for all His mercies, His love, and grace.

By: A. Walters

MOTHER TERESA'S THEME OF LIFE

by Albert Walters

Philippians 2:5 says, "Let this mind
be in you, which was also
in Jesus Christ." Do unto others as you would have them
do unto you. Love thy neighbor as thyself.

We are not alone! Oh blessed assurance,
Jesus is mine. Oh what a foretaste
of glory divine. 1 Corinthians 6:19-20.
"Do you know that your bodies are
temples of the Holy Spirit, who is in you,
whom you have received from God?
You are not your own; you were bought at
a price. Therefore, honor God with
your bodies."

Galatians 6:4, "let every man prove his
own works and then shall he have
rejoicing in himself alone and not in
another." Oh yes there is a crown and
we can win it, if we only walk in Jesus name.
I must have the Savior with me!

God please grant me the serenity to accept
the things I cannot change, courage
to change the things I can and the
wisdom to know the difference.

So I am somewhat convinced this was the
song Mother Teresa sung in closing:

"To be like Jesus - To be like Jesus - That's
all I ask - Is to be like Him - All
through life's journey - From earth to glory -
That's all I ask – Is to be like Him."

Blessed Be His Name.

What Qualities Are Desired In A Friend

- Albert Walters

Friendship is a priceless gift that cannot be bought or sold. But its value is far greater than a mountain made of gold. Well! To me a friend should be a trustworthy person, one that you can rely on and put your trust in. A worthy friend that can be emulated as a role model, loving and progressive minded. Such friends are treasures, priceless treasures desperately needed to rid us of this discombobulated situation we are faced with today, not knowing our enemies from our friends. O what a relief it would be to us all in so many ways, having this world rejuvenated with friends as citizens such as these, among us building our world of tomorrow. O this topic should have its resonances on our hearts and minds, in order for solidarity to have its full effect. Peace on earth and goodwill toward men should be our main objective in life. This world can be a much better place to live in, but we are lacking that unity - that peace - that generates genuine love needed to bond us more together as one and this is crunch time. Life can be beautiful dear friends, but it just endeavor awaits our positive response at work, at rest and at play throughout our life span. Through the guiding light of wisdom and understanding shall a family endure and children grow strong in the security of the home for they are the hope of the future Brothers and Sisters, the more we are together, the happier we shall be. God is coming back for his perfect world and would rather have it that way. Love always protects, always trust, always hope, always perserveres. Brothers and Sisters, beloved friends, big day dawns, love lifted me.

Good influence has always been my main objective from my much younger stage of life and I have all intensions of upholding that mindset pleasing to God, myself and my fellow man. Oh yes, I must give thanks to my great God, for this inspired heart and frame of mind making myself willing and available assisting my church missionaries in their door to door outreach program. As I minister to those lost souls, enlightening their hearts and minds, I hope I can make an impact on their lives to experience God's compassionate love towards them all. I hope I am able to influence them to see that His desire towards them is to enjoy a full life of prosperity. Well Brothers and Sisters life is a challenge by thy stripes thou shall be healed, let your theme of life be doing God's will. There is a crown and you can win it if you only walk in Jesus name. The more we are together the happier we shall be. God is coming back for His perfect world and would rather have it that way. Blessed are the peace makers for they shall be called Children of God, God is Love.

ALBERT WALTERS

Happy Tracts

With great enthusiasm I am writing on this topic, because of its impact on me. I can recall on my much younger days at school as a very good track and field athlete. My favorite events were the hundred yards dash and relay races. Being very conscious or aware of that trust and confidence placed on me, I would try and put out my best performance to please my friends and team mates for taking home that prestigious prize. Now, as I am older, I am now engaged with tracts evangelizing, reaching out to less fortunate ones spiritually.

Brothers and sisters beloved friends, metaphorically speaking this topic "happy tracts" motivates me greatly. O how sweet it is to be on the battle field for the Lord; being that willing and worthy inspired courageous humble servant He has ordained me to be fighting that good fight of faith with that prize of a higher calling in mind, knowing that Jesus is a winner man and greater is He that is in me, than he that is in the world. What have I to do now but go singing my happy songs?

BELOVED

Blend with us your voices!

O – to be like thee – O to be like thee – that's all I ask is to be like Him – all through life's journey – from earth to glory - that's all I ask is to be like Him.

Sailing on - as I go sailing on - sailing on – as I go sailing on - with Christ in the vessel – I'll smile at the storm – as I go sailing on.

O – I love Jesus - He is my Savior - Jesus Christ – loves me too.

Please let this mind be in you as it is in Christ Jesus, He is our friend and a mighty prayer answering God.

My Visit To The Garden.

Oh, what a pleasant day it was to be at the Brooklyn Botanic Gardens, on my first time there. I beheld such beautiful surprises, and how nicely kept they all were.

So many trees with welcoming voices of birds chirping and some singing. Oh! the Sensational Nightingales they out shined them all. One could not help to think, could these be angels or birds?

There were plants from various parts of the world and flowers boasting their new arrivals with their delicate, beautiful petals and aroma.

Oh, yes those fish ponds, they were all anxiously awaiting our arrival. Each one, as if busily swimming around in their various colors spreading the good news that we have finally arrived.

Written By: Riverway Member Albert Walters

2/7/11

IF THY LOVE BE MINE

If thy love be mine, I'd give praises; yea, I'd give endless
praises to my Lord and King for creating you;
And O, so good and true Thank Him for answering my
prayer, my fondest dream, my heart's desire.

Well Beloved, if thy love be mine, with a joyful heart I'd
cleave to
thee, and pledge to thee my life;
My heart an open book. Forever more this will be,
I'd ne'er decline one measure.

Mountains may crumble, empires may fall but beloved,
I wonder what fate could withstand our love,
If in Unity we stand what sound could I hear
That could thrill me more? What beauty could I behold
that could charm me more? For thou art
the fairest of ten thousand to my soul.

Precious thy stature and perfect thy frame shall ever remain

O, with an ember of thy love thou hast engraved on my heart a
song, a new song, a song that shall never grow old.
O, a song that blesses my soul.

If thy love be mine? That will be the day,
That'll be the day when I say "Goodbye world' I'm gone.
I'm gone to a new world a fairer world on high
Happy to be ever with my love." O, no other love have I.

God believes in you.
★★★★★★★★★★★★★★★

By A.W. Walters

Albert W Walters
897 Empire Boulevard Apt, B3
Brooklyn, N.Y.11213

President Barack Obama
The White House
1600 Pennsylvania Avenue
Washington, D.C. 20050

Dear President Obama:

I humbly beseech you, please give these few heart felt words of mine towards the Nation of Haiti your deepest compassionate thought. Please take to consideration their bleak unfortunate past history with their government. I wonder, would it be possible for you and the United Nations working together send them positive words of comfort?

I would like you both very much to work together to give them a brighter, and a much more durable, prosperous future. I am sure that it is feasible and would be a great lift to their spirits.

In closing how fitting it is to recall that everlasting blessing from God "Peace on earth and goodwill toward men." If God be for us, who can be against us? Standing firm in what we believe in and for all we stand for. I am positively sure that He will immensely bless all that participate.

This is a request to President Obama, asking him kindly to intervene in the unfortunate situation facing the Nation of Haiti.

Yours Truly,
Albert Walters

ALBERT WALTERS 5/9/11

Love Lifted me

Love o love o fervent love, please never let me go, please let thy Holy Spirit be ever seen manifesting in me by souls in need of a guide. O please grant me that spiritual strength I need to build on that faith, that trust and that confidence for serving you more willingly and worthily more fully in spirit and in truth. Being that willing and worthy inspired courageous humble servant you have ordained me to be. Love God's greatest gift to man is truly a great and wonderful thing, the more we pursue it in a Godly way, the more its intricacy is being highlighted and unfolded to those seeking his blessings and guidance. Oh yes, love is a treasure found in the most sacred part of our hearts. It forever blooms and grows by the river of aspirations and shines brightest on a dreary day.

My love ain't no ordinary love, it never fades never dies. Being driven by my burning yearning heart that desires for accomplishments the Godly way. Oh please, heavenly father Jesus, let my life be a light to some soul, and let thy Holy Spirit be ever seen manifested in me. When nothing else could help, love lifted me.

ALBERT WALTERS 10/11/11

Topic: Mothers Worth

Oh – yes, I must start by giving thanks and praises to my Lord and King, for creating you and, so - good and true. Mothers worth, O - this topic makes my happy heart sings.

Loving mothers what a wonder you are; loving mothers what a wonder you are; with your gentle love and affection you submits all attention; O - loving mothers what a wonder you are; – with your gentle love and devotion we have all need to submit to your protection; O - loving mothers we appreciate you; O - loving mothers we appreciate you.

You are all special to me, because I know you would have me do no wrong. For with you, although in this world of turmoil, rest assured there is always a brighter side somewhere. So I liken you all to a beautiful garden of flowers - in full bloom, that can

ALBERT WALTERS

Me And My Shadow

Oh – yes, this will make you laugh, listen up friends me and my shadow; we sure do make a formidable pair. Our theme of life is; we are on the battle field for the Lord. Despite our discrepancy of views, we sooner than later come to the same agreement.

Our agenda is really based on following up with the United Nations and NATO point's of view, towards atrocities and any immediate pressing situations within the country and around the world. This topic we know, will cause some mind boggling; but that's just what we had intended it to do. We are sincerely hoping to make an impact in the hearts and minds of governing officials and politicians of this world. We are really sick and tired of their doom and gloom policies in this day and age, which is supposed to be civilized. We are absolutely, totally, fed up with it.

Our hearts earnest quest is for God's will to be done in our lives; for us to live in peace and unity among our fellow men; and to have a God blessed durable inheritance for our future generation. Just as He had intended it to be. Well, there are higher heights and deeper depths to be pursued, so that's all for this edition. O God bless America, land that I love.

Albert Walters 10/11/11

JESUS

Oh, when I think of the goodness of Jesus and what he has done for me, my soul cries out, Hallelujah, thank God for saving me. Jesus, O precious Jesus, you mean so very much to me, thou lover of my soul. Please bless me with that spiritual strength I need to build on that faith, trust and confidence I have in you.

Being that willing and worthy, inspired, courageous, humble servant you have ordained me to be. Please also keep me in that frame of mind ever to be grateful unto you. O what a glorious day that will be, when we meet on that beautiful shore, where we all shall join in ceaseless praises, thanking you Jesus, thanking you Lord.

O build my mansion next door to Jesus, and tell the Angels I am coming home. O my sweet Rose of Sharon, you mean so very much to me, Oh yes, you are just all in all to me.

Choruses

Beloved lend us your voices

I must have Jesus - in my whole life – I must have Jesus - in my life - in my walking – in my talking - in my singing and my praying – yea - I must have Jesus - in my whole life.

O - with my hands lifted up - and my mouth filled with praise – with a heart of thanks giving – I will bless thee o Lord.

Oh! – if its only one song I can sing – this is the dearest that Jesus loves me – Oh!- I am so glad - - - that Jesus loves me – Jesus loves me – Jesus loves me - Jesus loves even - me.

WHAT'S MY PROBLEM

What's my problem?
Well, I guess they dissipate in the searing heat
of the sun,
2 Cor. 4:16-18   *The boisterous wind, the lightning of thunder,*
and the roaring seas
So they don't bother me.

What's my problem?
Well you see I believe in God, and for Him
Mat. 26:36   *a good ambassador I am striving to be.*
So that's why for me life is fun, life is free,
just as God had intended it to be, for me and
thee.

Oh where is He, where is my beloved,
My sweet Rose of Sharon who pleaded
Philip 3:14   *for me in Gethsemane and paid my debt on*
Calvary?
Oh who am I that a King should bleed and
die for?
And pleaded "not my will but thine" for? The
answer I
may never know why he ever loved me so, but
to that old
rugged cross. He went for me.

O sing it over again to me, that intriguing
love song the
song birds sing so well while the gentle breezes
tell their
stories they do so well.

41

Rev. 3:20

Oh! Who at my door is standing patiently drawing near,
entrance within demanding?
O whose the voice I hear?

By A.W. Walters

Printed in the United States
By Bookmasters